RHYTHM 'N' RHYME READERS

WHEN I GROW UP

Written by Babs Bell Hajdusiewicz
Illustrated by Steve Pileggi

Dominie Press, Inc.

WHEN I GROW UP

When I grow up,
who will I be
besides the person
who is ME?
I might bring mail.
I might play drums.
I might drive trucks.
I might grow plums.
I might fight fires.
I might trim trees.
I might type letters.
I might fix knees.
When I grow up,
I think I'll be a
worker who works
but I'll still be ME!